Right with God

RIGHT *with* GOD

LIFECHANGE BOOKS

RON MEHL

Multnomah®Publishers *Sisters, Oregon*

RIGHT WITH GOD

published by Multnomah Publishers, Inc.

© 2003 by Ronald D. Mehl, trustee

International Standard Book Number: 1-59052-186-2

Cover imge by Picture Quest

Unless otherwise indicated, Scripture quotations are from:
The Holy Bible, New King James Version © 1984 by Thomas Nelson, Inc.

Other Scripture quotations are from:
The Holy Bible, New International Version (NIV) © 1973, 1984 by International Bible Society,
used by permission of Zondervan Publishing House
New American Standard Bible® (NASB) © 1960, 1977 by the Lockman Foundation
The New Testament in Modern English, Revised Edition (Phillips) © 1958, 1960, 1972 by J. B. Phillips
The Living Bible (TLB) © 1971. Used by permission of
Tyndale House Publishers, Inc. All rights reserved.
Holy Bible, New Living Translation (NLT) © 1996. Used by permission of
Tyndale House Publishers, Inc. All rights reserved.

Multnomah is a trademark of Multnomah Publishers, Inc., and is registered in the U.S. Patent and
Trademark Office. The colophon is a trademark of Multnomah Publishers, Inc.

Printed in the United States of America

For information:
MULTNOMAH PUBLISHERS, INC.
POST OFFICE BOX 1720
SISTERS, OREGON 97759

Library of Congress Cataloging-in-Publication Data

Mehl, Ron.
    Right with God / Ron Mehl.
        p. cm.
Includes bibliographical references.
    ISBN 1-59052-186-2
    1. Ten commandments. 2. Christian life. I. Title.
BV4655 .M4332 2003
241.5'2--dc21   2002153766

03 04 05 06 07 08—10 9 8 7 6 5 4 3 2 1 0

CONTENTS

Chapter 1

ON EAGLES' WINGS

"You have seen what I did to the Egyptians,
and how I bore you on eagles' wings
and brought you to Myself."

EXODUS 19:4

JOYCE'S LOVE LETTERS always started out a little slow.

I was young, in college, in love, and in a hurry. And I couldn't help but note how her correspondence always moved along in low gear for the first few pages.

I wanted to jump right into the good stuff, to read the parts that said how wonderful I was. How she couldn't live without me. I could spend hours looking for code words and secret meanings.

I realize now that I would have enjoyed life a lot more if I'd just relaxed and treasured her letters for what they were. I really didn't need to read between the lines. The love was right there in front of me.

Have you ever heard the Ten Commandments described as a love letter from the hand of God? I'm convinced that they're one of the most powerful expressions of God's love in Scripture. He doesn't leave anything out. These ten statements are the truths He knows will provide blessing, strength, a future, and a hope.

Some people, of course, imagine the exact opposite. They don't hear love at all; they hear God saying, "You mess with Me and I'll fry you like a bug."

All this, of course, plays right into Satan's age-old caricature of God—the one he's had from the beginning. "God is a prude, a harsh old grandfather with a long beard and bushy eyebrows who doesn't want anyone to have any fun—ever."

Is he right? Are the Ten Commandments harsh and negative, or do they have a warmer, more passionate side?

To find out, let's begin with the words that set the Ten Commandments in context. Before God gave Moses those tablets of stone, He gave him specific instructions about what to say to the people before presenting the Ten Commandments. Can you hear His heart beating in these words?

> And Moses went up to God, and the LORD called to him from the mountain, saying, "Thus you shall say to the house of Jacob, and tell the children of Israel: 'You have seen what I did to the Egyptians, and how I bore you on eagles' wings and brought you to Myself. Now therefore, if you will indeed obey My voice and keep My covenant, then you shall be a special treasure to Me above all people; for all the earth is Mine. And you shall be to Me a kingdom of priests and a holy nation.'" (Exodus 19:3–6)

The Lord was saying, "Moses, before you give the people these commands, will you please remind them that I bore them on eagles' wings?"

What does that mean? Well, a mama eagle will make a nest at least eight feet by eight feet. The largest on record was more than nine feet wide and twenty feet deep. It weighed almost three tons.

She will fill it up with leaves, animal fur, and down from her own breast, so it's warm and snug. But when the time is right, she will make things uncomfortable for her unsuspecting little eaglets.

It all begins when she takes them to a "home" that will be more important to them than any nest in the world…the sky! She will pick them up, fly with them to a dizzying height, and drop them.

This is all shockingly new to the little eaglet. For him, life has been a comfy, snuggled-down, fuzz-ball existence, with little pals to play with, regular meals, and Mama's protective wings at night. But now Mama kicks him overboard, with nothing between him and certain death but the wild blue yonder.

Will you please remind them that I bore them on eagles' wings?

The eaglet begins to flutter. He doesn't know what to do. He doesn't even have a learner's permit. His heart pounds in his tiny chest. And he's heading down, fast.

As the little fella plummets to earth, contemplating his comfortable but surprisingly brief life, Mama Eagle watches. And what does she do? She swoops down just before her eaglet hits the ground and picks him up. And of course the poor little bird has gone into cardiac arrest. But there's a happy ending here for the baby eagle, right? Mom is climbing back into the heavens. Oh boy, the nasty trauma is over. Back to the beloved nest…and isn't it just about lunchtime?

But what does she do when she regains altitude? She drops him again! And again! And each time she swoops down to save him and bears him up...on eagles' wings.

That's exactly what the Lord is saying: "Moses, please—before you give them these commands, remind them how much I have loved them in the past. How I've watched over their lives every day and concerned Myself with their future."

We can look back on the same thing in our own lives, can't we? Everything we have and everything we enjoy are blessings from His hand. We, too, were headed south one day. But in Christ, the Lord swooped down and picked us up and gave us everything that we have. And now He sustains us and keeps us every day of our lives.

If we lose sight of that, we can't see anything at all. God is all about developing us and helping us grow. He loved the children of Israel. His purpose was to lead them step-by-step, test by test, so that when they crossed the Jordan they would have the faith and the strength to throw down walled cities and take possession of the land. He always has a plan!

He has a plan for you, too. Never doubt it. You might be puzzled by the circumstances and timing in your life, and you might feel that you're going nowhere fast. Yet God's eye is upon you. He will catch you on His wings and take you where you could never go in your own strength.

He carries you because He loves you. And that is what makes the Ten Commandments a love letter.

Chapter 2

NO OTHER GODS

"You shall have no other gods before Me."

EXODUS 20:3

RECENTLY I WAS AT A PASTORS RETREAT in a wilderness area in New England. A major snowstorm hit. One night one of the pastors slipped out of bed, put on snowshoes, and headed off for a walk with no flashlight, compass, or provisions.

He never marked his trail and paid no attention to landmarks. After a while he suddenly realized he was becoming very, very cold. And in that same instant he was jarred by another realization: *I have no idea how to get back!*

Others who searched for him that night eventually found him…cold, embarrassed, but none the worse for his midnight wanderings.

That's the deceptiveness of the path the world offers. It looks good until it suddenly dawns on you: *I don't know where I am! I've wandered into something and have no idea how to get back.* You're lost in the woods and it's too dark to retrace your own tracks.

King Solomon would have known the first command from boyhood. I suspect it was very much on his mind when he wrote these words: "Trust in the LORD with all your heart and lean not on your own understanding; in all your ways acknowledge him, and he will make your paths straight" (Proverbs 3:5–6, NIV).

That's pretty much the bottom line, isn't it? But notice that this statement is conditional. It tells us very specifically that we must not lean on or trust in our own understanding. Why? Because we are in a dangerous place full of traps and pits and swamps, and our compass is broken. Proverbs 14:12 says, "There is a way which seems right to a man, but its end is the way of death."

Yes, but don't these commands of God have a "stern" quality that sometimes puts us off? Perhaps…but when you are warning someone not to go where certain death awaits, how stern do you get?

Imagine that you take the winding drive up to

Glacier Point at Yosemite National Park. As you approach the top of the rock cliff, where you can peer over a belt-high railing at the valley 3,200 feet below, one of your car doors flings open and your three-year-old leaps out and begins running for the edge as fast as his chubby little legs will carry him.

We are in a dangerous place full of traps and pits, and our compass is broken.

Is it a time to whisper sweetly? Is it a time for a seminar on "values clarification"? No! As your heart lurches, you shout, "Tommy, stop! *Stop right now!*"

Do the Ten Commandments have a bit of that flavor? Do they seem written in bold with capital letters? Could it be because the Father heart of God lurches within Him as He sees spiritually blind, unheeding men and women running for the edge of the cliff?

Listen to the urgent tone of these words from Ezekiel:

> "As surely as I live, declares the Sovereign LORD,
> I take no pleasure in the death of the wicked,
> but rather that they turn from their ways and
> live. Turn! Turn from your evil ways! Why will
> you die, O house of Israel?" (Ezekiel 33:11, NIV)

It's as if the Lord were saying, "If you will acknowledge Me in all your ways, if you will hear and obey My word, I will keep you from harm and let nothing hinder your fulfillment."

He wants to care for you, and He knows that no one can care for you better than He can. Psalm 116 says that when we call upon Him, He inclines unto us. No matter where He's working or what project He's involved in, He leans over to hear us.

In verse 13 the psalmist says, "I will take up the cup of salvation, and call upon the name of the LORD." Here, "salvation" is not used as we mean it today. Old Testament believers didn't live in the shadow of the Cross. Salvation referred to the many times the Lord had sustained them and saved them from trouble. Their cups overflowed.

I have a cup like that, too, filled with the times God has helped me overcome doubt, disappointment, and failure. The times when He spared my life, kept our children from danger, and paid our bills. He has loved us and reached out to us and delivered us even when we were unlovely.

And now He is saying, "Knowing that I love you with a sacrificial, serving love, would you put Me first in your life, just as you are first in Mine?"

Many people ask me how I've dealt with years of leukemia—years of hanging by a rope over a cliff. But it's not so bad when you know who's holding the rope. My life really is His responsibility. He is responsible for the outcome. He is responsible for how long I live and serve. The weight is off me. He's responsible—and I'm not!

In fact, what you don't surrender is what ends up eating you alive, because you carry it and feel so responsible to bring it all to a good conclusion. Yet deep in your heart you know you never can.

What does Jesus say so clearly in Matthew 6? "Don't worry about anything. Don't worry about what you'll eat. Don't worry about what you'll wear or where you'll live. Don't fret over those things. Just seek Me first and everything will work out."

Worry is like a warning light on the dashboard, informing us that we've taken back our lives from His care—a very foolish thing to do.

I love the story about an eight-year-old boy taking a test. He became so nervous that he suddenly wet his pants. Horrors! He looked down and saw a little puddle. Sick with worry, he looked up just in time to see his teacher motioning him to her desk. How could he move? What could he do?

At that very moment, one of his classmates, a girl, came down the aisle from behind, carrying a large fishbowl. Suddenly she lurched and dropped the heavy bowl. It shattered with a loud crash and sent debris everywhere. Now covered by water, the boy sat there thinking, *Thank*

God! Thank God! There is a God in heaven!

But then it dawned on him that little boys don't like little girls. He couldn't possibly let this pass. "What's wrong with you, you clumsy clod? Can't you watch where you're going?!" As the class laughed, the teacher took the boy to the gym for dry clothes.

At lunchtime, no one sat with the girl. Her friends avoided her at recess. In the unforgiving society of elementary school, she was suddenly a plague and a pariah.

He knows that no one can care for you better than He can.

But when the day ended, the boy walked out the door and saw her. All the kids were leaving, but she was walking by herself. He reflected on what had happened and suddenly—on impulse—walked over to her.

"You know," he said, "I've been thinking. That wasn't an accident. You did that on purpose, didn't you?"

"Yes," she said. "I knew what had happened to you. I wet my pants once, too."

I heard this story and thought, *Lord, I don't want to ever forget what You have done for me. You covered me. You spilled Your precious blood and took all my shame on Yourself. You have fit me for heaven though I deserved hell. You have given me dignity and hope and a reason to get up in the morning.*

How could I not put such a God first?

Chapter 3

PURSUING
EMPTY IMAGES

*"You shall not make for yourself any carved image . . .
you shall not bow down to them nor serve them.
For I, the LORD your God, am a jealous God."*

EXODUS 20:4–5

HAVE I MENTIONED THAT I LOVE my wife Joyce very, very much?

I really do. We've been married more than thirty years now, and I'm as delighted with her today as when I was a Bible college preacher boy with stars in my eyes.

But tell me…how do you think she would like it if she saw my billfold lying open on our dresser and noticed a picture of another woman alongside hers? Do you think she would shrug her shoulders and say, "Well, this is interesting, but Ron has a right to his privacy"? Or do you think she might say, "Ron, who is this?"

And how do you think she would like it if she learned that this other woman and I had a bit of an ongoing relationship—that I turned to her when I especially needed affection and encouragement? Could you fault her for feeling jealous or hurt or angry over having to share my love and devotion with another?

Dumb question, huh? She's my wife. She has every right to expect and even insist that I keep myself for her alone. And you know what? I want to. Because of my love and my vows, I've always been a one-woman man.

I believe this to be the very spirit of the second commandment. Here's my sense of what the Lord is saying: "I am your God and Redeemer. I have saved you and bought you for Myself at a terrible price. Please…don't ever put anything in the place that belongs to Me."

Does this strike you as a little too restrictive? Too legalistic? Too much for the Lord to expect or require? Of course not. He is our God. What's the difference between a "carved image," a "graven image," and a photograph?

It's a love issue. It's a relationship issue. My wife doesn't want any rivals. My Lord doesn't either. His heart toward you and me does not change through the seasons and the years. What about our heart toward Him?

Every now and then I hear a man or woman utter *His heart toward you and me does not change through the seasons and the years.* some horrible words in my office. It's like a body blow each time: "Pastor, I just don't love my wife anymore." Or "I don't love my husband anymore." When that happens, I always ask myself, *Why? How could that be? What do they even mean by the word 'love'?*

I've been so troubled by this situation that I've changed the way I do premarital counseling. It's very typical for a couple to come into my office all calf-eyed, lovey-dovey, and wrapped about one another like vines. They can't seem to keep their hands or their eyes off each other, and I'm not sure they're hearing much of what I say.

In recent days I've been spoiling the party atmosphere by making them sit on opposite ends of the couch. Once I get them untwined and separated, I'll turn to the young man, look him straight in the eyes, and say, "Will you love this woman and serve her and care for her for the rest of your life? Are you prepared right now to say that the only thing you want from this relationship is to fulfill her, build her up, and satisfy her? Are you willing this moment to release your expectations? Are you marrying this woman because you believe you are God's gift to her?"

Now, this isn't usually what the young man is expecting. Some of the color drains out of his face, and he swallows hard. "Yes, Pastor," he croaks.

But I'm not done with him yet.

I then say, "Now, if you know that this is the will of God and that you're entering into this relationship not to receive, but to give everything, then I want you to remember this day. I don't want you coming to me five years from now telling me you 'don't love her.' Because I will know that you certainly did love her, and love isn't something you can trade in after a few years and fifty thousand miles. And I don't want you coming to me saying, 'This wasn't the will of God,' because we're sitting here today and we know that it certainly is the will of God."

These couples are hardly ever prepared for that sort of language, but I want them to understand that this relationship is for life.

Our relationship with the Lord is for life, too—and life beyond life. The commitment we make to Him is eternal, and God takes it very seriously. Matthew Henry says: "Since you know the true God, and are in Him.... Cleave to Him in faith, and love, and constant obedience, in opposition to all things that would alienate your mind and heart from God."

What, then, are those "images" in our world that would rise up to challenge our love relationship with the Son of God? What are the snapshots we might be tempted to frame on our desk, those "pictures in our wallet" that could gradually steal us away from a whole-hearted walk with Christ?

Jesus said to His disciples, "You cannot serve both God and Money" (Matthew 6:24, NIV). He was speaking of a spirit of materialism that grips the soul and demands our energies and devotion. Paul says in Colossians 3:5 that even greediness is idolatry. But Scripture might also have listed any of the other false gods of this world—power, pleasure, or status.

When it becomes the whole purpose of your life to chase one of those images, you have already slipped into idolatry. And when you worship a god, you basically surrender your life to it.

Our relationship with the Lord is for life, too—and life beyond life.

In the book of Acts, Paul was bewildered by the "many gods" that filled Athens. There must have been an idol on every block—as regular as fire hydrants. But what is that compared to today? The gods of materialism, sexual indulgence, and personal power fill the very airwaves! The images go across the world by satellite, cable, Internet, and slick printing. We are surrounded; they leer at us from billboards and call to us from television. And as every good advertising or network executive knows, the whole object is to "capture" as many people as possible.

How do false images affect us over the long haul? This is where Scripture makes some amazing statements.

Psalm 135 tells us:

The idols of the nations are but silver and gold, the work of man's hands. They have mouths, but they do not speak; they have eyes, but they do not see; they have ears, but they do not hear; nor is there any breath at all in their mouths. Those who make them will be like them, yes, everyone who trusts in them. (Psalm 135:15–18, NASB)

The clear fact is, we become like what we worship. And God knows that these false images will never satisfy our deeper thirsts or the longings of our hearts. As Jesus said to the woman at the well, "If you drink this water, you'll just be thirsty again. But there is a well—a well of living water—that could keep you from ever being thirsty again."

Our Father knows that the "images" offered by the world are bankrupt. He knows that if we pursue them, we will find ourselves disappointed and devastated because of what we've experienced. The false gods take, take, and take.

Recently I talked with a young woman. She was weeping, hands covering her face. "I've lost everything—" she said, "my virginity, my sense of value. Look at all these holes!" She had pierced herself for multiple rings in her ears and nose and mouth. "I'm twenty-one," she said, "and I don't want to live like this anymore. I thought it would be so good."

What this young woman was saying was simple. "Everything I reached for was a sham. Now who could ever love me?"

I then had the privilege of telling her about Someone who really did love her very much. Someone worthy of her faith and devotion, who loved her just the way she was and could someday make her shine with His reflected beauty and righteousness (see Philippians 2:15).

Someone we know as the One True God.

Chapter 4

TAKE CARE WITH THE NAME

*"You shall not take the name of the
Lᴏʀᴅ your God in vain."*

EXODUS 20:7

ONE OF MY FAVORITE PASTORAL DUTIES is dedicating little children and their parents. It's a delight to speak the names of the little ones before the congregation. Some come right out of the Bible…Jonah, Micah, Joshua, and David. I've prayed over Rachel, Ruth, and Mary. I've kissed Daniel, Esther, and Matthew on top of their downy little heads.

I know people who actually make a prophetic decision to name their children a certain name because of what it means. We certainly did with our boys. Ron Jr.'s name means "strong one." Mark's means "mighty warrior." Their names have become their character—or is it the other way around?

People's names represent something. God was so concerned about this fact that He actually named people Himself—or changed their names when their character changed. Think of Abram ("exalted father") to Abraham ("father of a multitude"), and Simon to Peter ("a rock").

So, if a name represents a person's character and is very important to God, why do so many people casually take the name of our heavenly Father and our Lord Jesus in vain?

We can sense why this might be an issue of deep concern to the Lord. But why would He make it one of the Ten Commandments? Is it possible that God knows something about what will happen to our lives if we become flippant about His name?

One definition of the word *profane* speaks of "debasing or defiling what is holy or worthy of reverence." It's an attempt to take something exalted or revered and jerk it down from its pedestal. When I profane something, I try to reduce it to nothing more than I am.

What does it mean, then, to profane the name of

God? It is nothing less than a denial of His holiness, majesty, and power. It is an attempt to somehow pull God down and make Him equal with us. And that is a grave and serious business.

I'll tell you how much honoring the name of God matters—He made it one of the Ten Commandments. Because He knows that every time we use those derogatory terms, incredible destruction comes into our lives. When you don't put God first and honor His name, life just doesn't work.

Names represent something— God actually named people himself.

I've heard men say, "G-D this home! G-D that woman! G-D those kids!" I don't think they have any awareness that these words and terms do not fall on deaf ears. In Matthew, Jesus warns us: "But I tell you that men will have to give account on the day of judgment for every careless word they have spoken" (Matthew 12:36, NIV). The Lord went on to say, "Your words now reflect your fate then: either you will be justified by them or you will be condemned" (v. 37, TLB).

My friend Jack Hayford tells about an incident when his family was out driving and Jack pulled into a little two-pump gas station. The attendant walked up, chewing on a toothpick. He greeted Jack warmly and began to fill the tank. As he did so he happened to look down at the tires.

"You know," he told Jack, "your G-D tire is about to blow. If it does, you and your family will have a wreck. If I were you, I'd get a new tire."

Jack said, "Could you please take care of that?"

"Sure can," the man replied.

And while this man worked on the car, it seemed to Jack that every other word was G-D this and G-D that. This G-D car and these G-D tires and those G-D highways.

Finally, Jack couldn't take any more. "Sir, I don't want God to damn my car. I wish you wouldn't say that."

The man looked startled. "Oh," he said. "I'm sorry."

Jack said, "You know, sir, you work with tires, and you spared my family from an accident—and I'm grateful. But I'm a pastor. I work with souls. And when I heard you talking like that, I thought, *He spared my family from disaster; I want to spare him from disaster.* You need to know that using God's name in vain is a very expensive thing. You can't do it and not pay a price."

The problem with most people is that they use God's name any way they want and think they "get away" with it. Yet you never reap in the same season you sow. God's Word is true. Using His name in vain will affect your life.

There is power in the name of God. There is power in the name of Jesus Christ. Demons screamed and tore themselves from their hosts at the mention of His name.

In the authority of His name, the eyes of the blind were opened, withered legs were made strong, and dead bodies came out of the grave.

When we use the name of God in a careless way and call on Him to "damn" or condemn something, we set something in motion beyond our finite understanding. David said, "For You, O God, have heard my vows; You have given me the heritage of those who fear Your name" (Psalm 61:5).

The problem with most people is that they use God's name any way they want and think they "get away" with it.

David is saying that God brings all those who fear, love, and honor His name into the heritage of those who have honored His name down through the years. It is a heritage of blessing and honor, of fruitfulness and joy.

How could we dishonor the very source of all honor and blessing? For that matter, how can we stand by silently while His name is being dragged through the mud? How can we go on watching a movie or reading a book where His name is deliberately defamed?

People may say, "Well, I just grew up around a certain kind of talk." Yet Scripture always links what comes out of our mouths with our hearts. Jesus Himself said this again and again. It was important enough to Him to repeat.

- "You brood of vipers, how can you who are evil say anything good? For out of the overflow of the heart the mouth speaks." (Matthew 12:34, NIV)
- "But the things that come out of the mouth come from the heart, and these make a man 'unclean.'" (Matthew 15:18, NIV)
- "The good man brings good things out of the good stored up in his heart, and the evil man brings evil things out of the evil stored up in his heart. For out of the overflow of his heart his mouth speaks." (Luke 6:45, NIV)

Like it or not, the mouth speaks what is in the heart. The way you talk is because of your heart, and the Lord knows that. You cannot say, "Well, she has a vile mouth but a good heart." Or, "He's got a problem with bad language, but he really does have a heart of gold."

Beyond that, there are other ways to use His name in vain—socially acceptable ways to profane Him. I have been guilty and perhaps you have, too. One way is to be very casual, or careless, in our prayers. The Lord cautions us against "vain repetitions." Vain means empty, saying things over and over, without conviction.

Others twist Scripture and say, "When you come to the Lord, just ask for whatever you want. A bigger house, a new car, a better job. Then when you're done, just say, 'in Jesus' name, amen,' and you'll get it!"

How should you respond when you realize you've taken the Lord's name in vain? I suggest three simple steps.

1. RECOGNIZE SIN AND CONFESS IT.

Confession means "to speak the same as." It means, "Lord, I agree with You." Tell Him you're sorry you used His name in vain. If you do, He will wash your heart clean.

2. ACCEPT HIS FORGIVENESS.

Just tell Him, "Lord, there is so much disarray and confusion in my life, my home, and my business. I have not honored Your name. I have not entered into the heritage of those who fear Your name.

3. PRACTICE GOD'S PRESENCE.

Remember, He's always there. He hears, sees, and knows everything. If I used God's name in vain and my boys heard me, at the very least I'd be teaching them to be casual about the presence of God. Maybe even giving them permission to *openly dishonor* their heavenly Father. On the contrary, I want them to know that He not only sees and hears, but also *cares*. And I want them to care equally, in return.

Chapter 5

A TIME
TO REFLECT

"Remember the Sabbath day, to keep it holy."

EXODUS 20:8

I WOKE UP IN THE ICU as a familiar face swam into focus.

It was my dear friend Jack Hayford, and even in my medicated state I knew that expression. Jack loves me very much, but I had a hunch he hadn't flown up from Los Angeles to quote poetry.

"Good enough for you?" he asked.

What kind of greeting was that? What a strange

thing to say to a friend after a near-fatal heart attack. But Jack was just warming up.

"You're a prideful man, Ron. You think people are really impressed that you work seven days a week."

I groaned. He'd said the same thing many times before, but I'd always run to another appointment or changed the subject. Now I was stuck in a hospital bed, shackled by tubes and IVs. I could pretend to fall asleep, but I had a feeling Jack wouldn't buy it.

"This is an ego thing for you, isn't it, Ron? You want affirmation. You want everybody to say, 'Isn't he amazing? Works seven days a week.' Get serious, Mehl! Who are you trying to impress? God? Well, I can tell you He's only impressed with one thing, and that's His Son."

Jack had certainly earned the right to speak to me that way. What's more, I knew that he was right. I knew I had violated one of God's life principles, and I was paying the price.

There's no use denying it; I've struggled with this fourth command. I've had trouble understanding why this Sabbath thing should even be one of "The Ten." Sure it's important. But alongside murder and adultery—come on! Why does the Lord say a Sabbath rest is so important? I have resisted this fourth command-ment…and I have paid for that resistance.

In fact, very dearly.

I'm not saying that everyone who ignores the Sabbath will have a heart attack and wake up to find Jack Hayford in his face. But I am saying that if you consistently dishonor the Sabbath principle, somewhere along the line the bills will come due.

Why does the Lord say a Sabbath rest is so important?

Others besides Jack had warned me strongly before the heart attack. I had a nagging sense of conviction, too. I knew I should be carving time out of my dawn-to-dark schedule—more time with the Lord, with Joyce, with the boys; more time to rest my body and mind. But I just didn't do it. I put it off.

I've pastored the same church for thirty years. And through the years, for countless weeks at a time, I have been there seven days a week. But the heart attack—and some other bone-jarring bumps in the road—were a stern reprimand from God. He was telling me, "I love you, son, but these are not the Ten Suggestions."

Yet there are so many needs! So much hurt. So many open doors. I keep wrestling with the idea that God "needs" more of me to get His work done.

And yet, the truth is, I need more of Him. As demands on me go through the roof, I need more of His peace, His joy, His tenderness, His tough love, His wisdom; more of His resurrection life flowing through me.

And He won't give it to me in one-minute bursts between appointments.

He wants a relationship.

During my days of recuperation, I sensed the Lord saying, "Son, if you continue to run from Me on this, there will be more breakdowns. I didn't build you to work seven days a week. I didn't work seven days either! If you think you can live your life without letting Me renew and restore you, you are mistaken—and I am not pleased!"

Remember what David sang about the Lord?

The Lord is my shepherd;
I shall not want.
He makes me to lie down in green pastures;
He leads me beside the still waters.
He restores my soul. (Psalm 23:1–3)

Please note that "He makes me to lie down" comes before "He restores my soul." Restoration is neither quick nor cheap.

By the way, Jack Hayford didn't leave my bedside that day with those hard words still floating in the air. He sat down with his hand on mine, and there were tears in his eyes. "Ron," he said gently, "I believe

He wants a relationship.

God is telling you that if you will honor the Sabbath principle, God will fulfill the mighty plan He's purposed for you."

Our Lord gave these principles to us in love, for our protection. So, if you're not in sync with that, maybe the Lord wants you to ask some questions.

Is He really first in your life? Is there anything between you and Him? When you're lonely and feeling empty, is He the one you seek?

OF SHOES AND SOILS

My wife Joyce recently enlightened me with the news that if you wore a new pair of shoes every day, they would last about six months. But she went on to theorize that if you alternate two pairs of shoes every other day, both pairs will last about two years.

What's the difference? Because the leather has a rest, it lasts significantly longer.

I might have doubted her if not for something I learned twenty-four years ago. There was a bowling alley a few blocks from our church. As I visited with one of the guys who worked there, I learned something amazing. Every couple of weeks, this bowling establishment removed all their pins from service and put them on a shelf, alternating them with another set. Do you know why?

So the bowling pins could rest.

"Come on! You're just pulling my leg! Bowling pins need to rest?"

He swore it was true. They apparently discovered that if the wooden pins don't rest, they won't bounce around as much or be as "alive." All of that flipping and knocking around eventually takes a toll. But if you give them a couple of weeks off and set them in a corner, they'll come back with more life than ever.

How do you top that? Well, my friends in agriculture tell me that even dirt needs to rest. Farmers don't plant the same things in the same fields year after year. They may plant corn one year and beans the next, on the same ground.

Why? Because the corn will take certain nutrients out of the soil, and the beans will put 'em back. A good farmer will let whole tracts of ground lie fallow for a year or more. Because the land benefits from the rest. After a time of lying easy, it yields a more bountiful crop.

Imagine that! Exodus 20:11 says that in six days the Lord made the heavens and earth, the sea, and all that is in them, and rested on the seventh day. Do you think the Lord might have some insights into His own creation? Do you think He might know something about you and me that we tend to forget?

Perhaps God is also saying, "You know, I am

extremely busy up here. I'm working all over, keeping things in order and holding things in place. And you're busy with lots to do, too. But would it be possible that maybe one day a week we could set aside some time because of our love for one another? Could we have one day where we could just talk and be with one another?"

I think that's what God had in His heart with this fourth commandment. God knows that if we get so busy and ahead of ourselves that we don't have time for Him, we'll simply wear out, years before He intended.

I also believe God gave the fourth commandment with a special kind of intimacy in mind. I've heard intimacy described as into-me-see. It is a point in my journey where I slow down enough so that the Lord can look into my life and see how I'm doing, and how I'm not doing…what needs to be touched…where the spiritual shoes of my life are wearing thin. (See Psalm 139:23–24).

But this intimacy implies more that the Lord looking into my heart. Wonder of wonders, I get to look into His heart and life and see Him, too. He desires that I do so.

Friendship with God is reserved for those who reverence Him.

Chapter 6

A COMMAND
WITH A PROMISE

"Honor your father and your mother."

EXODUS 20:12

I STOOD NERVOUSLY AT THE DOOR and looked into a face I had never seen before. Not even in a picture. Not even in my imagination. Yet it was like looking in a mirror. Forty-some years of questions and apprehensions tumbled about in my mind. This was the first time I could ever remember seeing my father.

He invited Joyce and me into his tiny apartment. We hugged; he wept a little. We made an awkward attempt at small talk. He was very careful to take the blame for our family's breakup. He'd gone away to the war, he told us in a quiet, hesitant voice. And when he came back to his wife and new baby, "Things weren't the same."

He looked into my eyes. "I know," he said slowly, "that you can never forgive me."

"Then I guess you really don't know me," I replied.

This encounter with my biological father took place some years ago, after a nationwide search. It was Joyce's idea. She had felt even more deeply than I that something in my life remained unfinished. So I agreed, she found him, and we packed our bags for his home in Minnesota. For me, meeting my father would be living out the fifth commandment in a way I had never imagined.

If you had a list of the Ten Commandments evenly spaced on a sheet of paper, the fifth commandment would be just above the middle. I don't think that was an accident. I believe these words are central to the Ten and to life itself. In many ways, our destiny hinges on how we respond. It affects our future, our past, and our "right now"—what God will do in our lives today.

Notice, also, that this command is the only one with a promise attached:

"Honor your father and your mother, that your days may be long upon the land which the LORD your God is giving you." (Exodus 20:12)

Here again, so very clearly, we can see the operative principle behind the Ten Commandments—God's abiding love for us. They truly are the tender commandments.

Why should we honor our father and mother? So that we might live. So that we might not be taken captive by bitterness. So that we might enjoy God's good gifts to us through all the days of our lives. The Lord is saying, "If you will honor the father and mother that I gave you, things will be well with you. I will honor, bless, and extend your life."

My own father and mother went their separate ways when I was a baby. Like many others that I've counseled over the years, I have had to face the pain and the emptiness of having a dad who wasn't there for his little boy. My mother never mentioned his name to me in her whole life.

Worst of all, I had to work through the feelings of rejection that began to surface in my adolescence. Maybe it was all because of me. Maybe I was the reason....

Through the years it's been an exercise of faith for me to find ways to honor this man in my words and my heart.

But that's never been the case when I've thought about Mom. Preaching at her funeral a few years ago was truly one of the highlights of my life. It was truly a joy to honor her memory before those who gathered at the service.

Not long after she died, I sat in her trailer house and looked up at the old roasting pan she used when I was five or six years old. In her kitchen drawer was the same spatula that she used to serve cake and fudge. She even had the same jewelry— tiny brooches that had one or two red or green rhinestones missing.

How much do you want the Lord to use your life?

I loved her old-fashioned gospel. I can still hear her testifying in church. She believed that to be saved and sanctified was to be "set apart" for God's special use. Even her pots and pans were sanctified, one for roast and one for cake and fudge. As far as she was concerned, a young man named Ron Mehl was also set apart. "Son," she'd tell me, "set your life apart for God's work, and He'll bless you greatly."

Obviously, I was very blessed to have a mom who loved the Lord and loved me very much. Yet you may be reading this chapter and thinking, *This command doesn't apply to me, because I don't have the kind of parents who should be honored. If this Mehl guy knew the scars I bear and the grief and abuse I've been through, there's no way in the world he would apply this commandment to me.*

But the Lord didn't list any exceptions, exemptions, or special considerations. It applies to all of us. And please hear this: No matter what has happened to us in the past, God is interested in our right now.

He wants to change your heart and mine right now, not tomorrow. He wants to walk with us and fellowship with us right now. Not later on, after we "get things straightened out." He wants to teach us and bless us right now, not on some mythical day when we "have our act together."

And right now, if you settle this matter of honoring your parents, you can be a different person. A son or daughter who forgives from the heart can be a different kind of parent to his or her own children, a parent—and a child—that the heavenly Father can bless in unimaginable ways.

No, God doesn't close His eyes or ignore the pain parents sometimes inflict on their own children. He holds them accountable. In Matthew 18:6 (NASB), the Lord Jesus said very sternly, "But whoever causes one of these little ones who believe in Me to stumble, it is better for him that a heavy millstone be hung around his neck, and that he be drowned in the depth of the sea."

Yet even knowing and understanding these things more deeply and intimately than you and I ever could in a lifetime, His Word still teaches us: "Honor your father and mother...that it may go well with you" (Ephesians 6:2–3, NIV).

So how, then, do we do that?

BY LOVING THEM

Love, someone said, is best spelled *T-I-M-E.* You love someone when you spend time with that person. "Well," you say, "I don't really care to spend time with my parents. I think they love making me feel miserable."

That may be. Honoring them by your presence may be difficult. Tracking down my father and flying across the country wasn't easy for me. There were times when I felt I'd rather face another chemotherapy treatment. But I needed to obey the Lord.

A heart free of bitterness, full of forgiveness, is a great place for the Lord to begin His work.

Maybe you'd love to spend more time with your parents but they live far away. Yet it's been said that you only really love someone when you sacrifice for them. The Lord sacrificed His Son. One of the best ways to show our love for our parents is to endure some inconvenience for their sakes. And God is well pleased.

But there are certainly other ways when travel is impossible. It may be as simple as a handwritten note, even when it's not a birthday or a holiday. Or picking up the phone in the middle of the day and saying, "How's it going? I was thinking about you...."

BY FORGIVING THEM

Now that I'm over half a century old, I've finally discovered something. In most cases, my mom did what she thought was right when she was raising me. At the time, I thought, *You're being too hard on me. You just want to make my life miserable.* Now I realize she usually knew a few things I didn't.

But you say, "Ron, you have no idea what I've been through. You don't know what you're talking about."

No, I really don't know what you've been through. But I do know something of what Jesus went through. When it comes to forgiveness, never forget this: The innocent party almost always pays. The one who has been offended is usually the one who must pay the price. But the one who forgives will also experience the mighty blessings of God on his life. How do you calculate the value of that?

That day I finally met him, I remember looking at my dad and saying, "If the Lord has forgiven me after all I've done, how could I ever hold anything against you? Dad, listen to me. I don't know everything about the past, but I forgive you."

When I said those words, tears sprang to his eyes. I could almost hear the sounds of a key turning in a lock and a jail door swinging open. I watched him experience release in that moment.

And in a strange way, I guess I did, too. I sensed a completion in my own heart in an area that had long been under lock and key. To my knowledge I hadn't held any bitterness, but that part of my heart had been shoved into the bottom of a Deepfreeze. At that moment, the frost melted.

Just six months later, he passed away.

It all comes down to this: How much do you want the Lord to use your life? How available do you really want to be when the Holy Spirit comes looking for someone to use? A heart free of bitterness and full of forgiveness and honor is a great place for the Lord to begin His work.

Chapter 7

REMOVING THE
SEEDS OF MURDER

"You shall not murder."

EXODUS 20:13

GOD KNOWS VERY WELL how far humanity has fallen.

He knows what kind of world this has become because of man's rebellion. You and I react with shock to stories of murder and mayhem, but none of it is "news" to Him. He knew this morning's news last night and knows what the headlines will be tomorrow.

God also knows that men and women will simply destroy themselves when the evil in their hearts goes

47

unchecked. That is why, when He met with Moses on the mountain before the nation of Israel, He included these four weighty words among His ten commands: "You shall not murder."

Now, you might be saying, "I've never murdered anyone, and I've never committed adultery, so why am I wasting my time with this stuff?" But before you check out on me, hear what Jesus had to say:

> "You have heard that it was said to those of old, 'You shall not murder,' and whoever murders will be in danger of the judgment. But I say to you that whoever is angry with his brother without a cause shall be in danger of the judgment. And whoever says to his brother, 'Raca!' shall be in danger of the council. But whoever says, 'You fool!' shall be in danger of hell fire." (Matthew 5:21–22)

Saying "Raca!" (empty-head) and "Fool!" to someone comes close to writing off that person altogether. What we're really saying is, "This person doesn't deserve to be alive...and I really wouldn't mind pushing him over the edge."

That is murder in the heart. And that is where it all starts.

So how does this sixth commandment reflect the love of God? In what way is "You shall not murder" one of His tender commandments?

Because He knows that when we love Him above all else and put Him first, we will not injure anyone. It will not be in our hearts to offend, humiliate, or destroy. We will have His heart toward others.

God knows that we will simply destroy ourselves when the evil in our hearts goes unchecked.

But what about the blind, empty-headed fools of the world? What about those who have made themselves our enemies?

We will love them. Just as He loved us and went to the cross for us when we were fools and enemies of God.

What, then, is the real source of this commandment? What causes people to murder? According to Jesus, murder begins with seeds of hatred and anger that take root in our hearts. We say, "If looks could kill…" But in a sense, they can. Anger and hatred are murderous things; they distort us so that our very faces reflect death.

But Scripture has this counsel: Ephesians 4:26–27 (NIV) says, "'In your anger do not sin': Do not let the sun go down while you are still angry, and do not give the devil a foothold."

Never forget: Your soul has a bitter adversary who wants to see such disaster in your life. Unresolved anger draws Satan to you like raw meat draws a shark. And he will devour your marriage and your family if you let those seeds of murderous anger take root.

If you have any doubts, you have only to go back and see what transpired in the very first family. When the Lord looked with favor on Abel's offering, but not on Cain's, Cain became angry.

> Then the LORD said to Cain, "Why are you angry? Why is your face downcast? If you do what is right, will you not be accepted? But if you do not do what is right, sin is crouching at your door; it desires to have you, but you must master it." Now Cain said to his brother Abel, "Let's go out to the field." And while they were in the field, Cain attacked his brother Abel and killed him. (Genesis 4:6–8, NIV)

How much God loves us! He tried to reassure and comfort this disappointed, angry man. And finally, He gave him a serious warning. But Cain had nurtured the anger and bitterness in his heart so long that he walked right around God to kill his only brother.

As in all the issues of our lives, Jesus deals with the root of this commandment, not just the fruit. He is not content to trim the nettles close to the ground. He wants to uproot the whole weed. And He tells us that the root of murder is hateful, people-dishonoring anger.

As always, the Lord wants to talk about internal things. He wants to talk about what's really happening in our hearts. And He knows that long before we would end someone's life we might begin the process with thoughts, then take it further with words.

Don't entertain any false notions. Words do hurt. Words can kill. In fact, contrary to what my mother told me, words not only break bones, they crush bones. They can wipe a smile off a face. They can steal hope from a heart. They can quench those little sparks of fun and joy and tenderness that make life worth living.

The Lord wants to talk to us about what's really happening in our hearts.

Let me tell you about a strikingly beautiful lady who went to her pastor for counseling. She told him that she was having difficulty responding romantically to her husband because, "I'm so unattractive."

The pastor thought to himself, *You've got to be kidding!*

So she told this story. As a teenager, acne covered her face. She had crooked teeth and wore Coke-bottle glasses. But an amazing thing happened. She turned fourteen and began to develop faster than other girls her age. One day while she was on her way to school, the big man on campus saw her, and he spoke to one of his friends so she could overhear him.

"Woo-eee. Look at her! Put a bag over her head and she'd be terrific."

In time she outgrew the bad complexion. Braces straightened her teeth, and contact lenses replaced the thick glasses. She became a beautiful woman, and everyone knew it.

Everyone but her.

The words that young man so carelessly spoke had crushed her spirit and strangled any feelings of self-worth she might have developed. Twenty-five years later she was still thinking, *All I really need to be attractive is a big bag over my head.*

Hateful words and unresolved anger also destroy the ones who harbor them in their hearts. Hate and anger are murderous, and like a two-edged sword they always cut in both directions. Let God deal with both.

Don't "murder" the ones He loves…including yourself.

Chapter 8

GOD'S FENCE
AROUND
YOUR MARRIAGE

"You shall not commit adultery."

EXODUS 20:14

HAVE YOU EVER WATCHED a rider on the back of a Brahma bull? When that bull swings his massive head and shoulders and sends the rider into the sawdust, the cowboy's natural instincts kick in and he begins to run. He heads toward the fence as fast as he can go, wishing—for a second or two, maybe—that it wasn't there. But after putting that barrier between himself and two thousand pounds of rage, he feels pretty good about that old fence. He might even lean over and give it a kiss.

Why should a rodeo cowboy love a fence? Because the fence isn't there to restrain the rider; it's there to restrain the bull.

The fence isn't there to restrain the rider; it's there to restrain the bull.

That's what God's commandments do for us. They put a barrier between us and that which would destroy us. They place a restraint on flesh that wants what it wants at any cost.

In one of C. S. Lewis's Chronicles of Narnia classics, two children are presented with a dilemma while exploring a strange, ancient world. In the crumbling ruins of a once-great palace, they come across a beautiful golden bell. Lying beside it is a tiny golden hammer. Below it is a sign. At first the children can't read the letters, but slowly the words reform into English:

Make your choice, adventurous Stranger;
Strike the bell and bide the danger,
Or wonder, till it drives you mad,
What would have followed if you had.[1]

Polly shrinks away from the bell. She wants nothing to do with the danger. But Digory, the boy, is seized with an insatiable curiosity. Before Polly can stop him, he grabs the hammer and strikes the bell. It immediately produces a clear, sweet note. But rather than fading, the sound of the bell grows and grows, until it becomes deafening. Walls and buildings begin to collapse under the massive reverberation, and the children barely escape with their lives. Digory's impulsive decision brings tragedy beyond anything he could have imagined.

People say, "I can do what I want to do. It's my life. I can live the way I want to. Maybe God does say, 'Don't commit adultery,' but it's really none of His business."

Yet it is His world and it is His business. He loves people like you and me so much that He made a list of restrictions to protect us from things that would destroy our lives and those of the people we love.

Adultery is one of those things. And as with the bell in Lewis's book, the consequences of adultery roll on and on, growing in their destructive intensity and affecting generation after generation.

Why should purity and faithfulness in a marriage be so important to God? Because He ordained the home and the church to visibly model His love. It is in Satan's interest to disfigure both of those models. In particular, Satan seeks the destruction of married love and the family.

I don't watch much TV, but I've seen enough to

know that on any given evening you will encounter a constant parade of suggestive sexual encounters. Virtually every program is riddled with immorality, seduction, and flirtation.

It's adultery, plain and simple. But Hollywood has made it appear so exciting, fulfilling—and even funny. The image makers surround it with laughter, beautiful music, and sumptuous settings.

People who witness these make-believe encounters begin to think, *My life is so dull. So unromantic. Where is the music and laughter? Maybe this will fill that gaping hole in my heart.*

But those who spin these silky, perfumed myths never show you what follows in real life. The movie versions of the David and Bathsheba story don't bother with the death and devastation. David's an impressive hulk and she's Miss Israel. It's always silk sheets, marble tubs, and a palace. But they never tell you what happened in the remaining years of David's life, the tortured history of his shattered family.

He made a list of restrictions to protect us from things that would destroy our lives.

Satan reminds me of the kind of used car salesman who only cares about that one sale. He says, "What can I do to get you into this car today?" You say, "Well, it's nice, but I need to go home, talk to my family, and look at my budget." And he replies, "No, no, you need to buy this car now. I can make it all possible for you. You'll never see a deal like this again. You deserve this. You need this. Here—I'll get the papers ready."

Satan doesn't want us to think beyond "now." He doesn't want us to look down the road. He doesn't want us to think about the payments we will make for the rest of our lives.

WHERE ADULTERY BEGINS

Some will say, "I've never committed adultery and never would. This is a waste; it doesn't apply to my life!"

Really? What about Jesus' words in Matthew 5:27–28?

> "You have heard that it was said to those of old,
> 'You shall not commit adultery.' But I say to you
> that whoever looks at a woman to lust for her
> has already committed adultery with her in his
> heart."

Where else does adultery begin, if not in the mind? The truth is, there is no such thing as a one-night stand. An affair begins to play itself out on the stage of imagination long before it occurs in real life.

The real battle is the battle of the mind. That's where

it began with Eve, and that's where the battle has raged ever since. Satan begins to whisper in your ear, and you find yourself thinking about what you want, what you "need," and what (by all "rights") you should have.

When God says, "Heed My Word," we need to remember that He has watched countless people walk across this planet. He has watched the pain and trouble that have come from every violation of this seventh commandment. How could a loving God do less than warn us? How could He do less than set His protective fences down across the landscape of our lives and urge us to walk safely within them?

Chapter 9

LETTING GOD
MEET YOUR NEEDS

"You shall not steal."

EXODUS 20:15

AT ONE END OF THE SCALE, you have unprincipled men like Charles Keating, who wiped out the savings of thousands of investors in a multimillion-dollar savings-and-loan swindle.

At the other end, you have Ron Mehl and a candy machine.

I was attending a convention years ago, staying in a hotel and feeling lonely. In the middle of the night I walked down the hall to find a vending machine. If I couldn't be with Joyce, I could at least buy a Snickers bar.

I dropped my coins, pushed the button, and waited for my candy. But nothing came out. *Great,* I thought, *just great.* Frustrated, I hauled off and hit the machine. Immediately, ten Snickers bars dropped out, along with my coins.

When I saw all that loot, I thought, *Oh boy, God really does provide!* I thought of Joseph's brother, Benjamin, getting a sackful of grain and his silver back besides. Being a spiritual young man, I reasoned, *I can tithe this. Maybe that's why God showered me.* I would dedicate one candy bar to the Lord and eat the other nine.

I took my stash back to the room and ate one of the "free" bars. But even though Snickers has always been my favorite, this one didn't taste very good. I ate it kind of fast, then began to feel guilty. To console myself, I ate another. By the time I'd finished that one, I felt like a crook. I didn't sleep much that night.

The next morning I confessed, first to the Lord and then to the manager at the front desk. The Lord heard me right away, but the manager didn't really want to be bothered. It was a hassle for him. He'd have to tell the candy guy and keep the contraband lying around.

"Come on," he said. "You've got to be kidding. Just take what you have and forget it. Call it your lucky day."

Not a chance. That manager was either going to deal with my stolen loot or have me stand there all day looking at him. When I finally got it all settled, I went and enjoyed my breakfast. Unlike the candy, the bacon and eggs did not stick in my throat.

I wonder how Charles Keating enjoyed his breakfasts. I remember watching television coverage on the savings-and-loan swindler. He was sentenced to twelve years and seven months in prison, but then went free on a technicality.

This man siphoned millions of dollars from a legitimate Savings and Loan into high-risk financial schemes that went bust. Most of the investors were retired, and they lost more than 285 million dollars—their life savings wiped out instantly.

I watched his sentencing on television. The defense team brought in his children and grandchildren. They wept before the judge. "Please don't sentence our father and grandfather like this. He's a good man. But if he goes to prison, he'll die there, and we won't get to grow up with him. Please don't do this to him."

Do you think Mr. Keating ever thought for a moment about those consequences? Did the candy he bought with all that money ever stick in his throat? Did he ever visualize such a tearful courtroom scene?

The eighth commandment is about taking something

that doesn't belong to you. And yes, it applies equally to financial assets and vending machine candy.

How do people end up stealing? Some do it knowingly. They borrow money, knowing very well they'll never pay it back. Some steal in more subtle ways, perhaps robbing from their employers by habitually taking long lunch breaks. I tease Joyce about doing that in her work at the church. But then again, we don't pay her, so I guess we can't complain too much.

By the time I'd finished, I felt like a crook.

Why would the Lord make "Do not steal" one of the Ten? I actually went to the Lord to ask. *Lord,* I prayed, *I believe every one of these commands pertains to Your love for us. They are tender commandments. But how does this demonstrate love?*

The answer hit me hard. "I don't want you stealing because I am the One who will supply all your needs. I don't want you to scheme, manipulate, and deceive to obtain things. What would you then become? I don't want you to feel responsible for securing your own future."

The truth is, every time we steal something, large or small, we are saying, "I will be my own provider. And if I don't take it now, I will lose."

But when we place our trust fully in Him, we never

lose. Through this commandment the Lord said, "Let Me provide for you. I want you to trust Me, rest in Me, and be content with Me."

The Lord has given us, as Peter says, "great and precious promises" (2 Peter 1:4, NIV). He has pledged Himself to satisfy and supply our every need.

So why do people steal?

BECAUSE THEY WANT INSTANT HAPPINESS

God understands this motivation, as He understands all of Satan's traps. The deceiver convinces us that taking something now will give us an immediate lift and will fill the voids in our lives—which, of course, can only be filled by the Lord Himself.

In His tenderness, God wants to spare us from the humiliation and damage that stealing can do to the people we love. In His mercy, He wants to shield us from the curse this activity brings upon our lives.

Proverbs 15:16 says, "Better is a little with the fear of the LORD, than great treasure with trouble."

BECAUSE THEY WANT SECURITY

People find their security in amazing ways. I heard of one man who literally filled his garage, floor to ceiling, with Styrofoam ice chests stuffed with rolls of toilet paper. He figured, I suppose, that in a world crisis he'd have enough if the stores ran out. For this man, that represented security!

People sometimes think, *If I can just grab this, it will give me the security I'm longing for.* They think riches and "things" will make them happy. But money and possessions are no security at all! All the money that you possess by deception will fly away. God also knows that the very things we pursue to secure the future will fall short. A lingering illness can erase a life's savings. A house full of possessions can be wiped out by a flood—or swept away by an IRS audit.

I am the One who will supply all your needs.

The only thing secure in this life is God. As David said, "I have set the LORD always before me. Because he is at my right hand, I will not be shaken. Therefore my heart is glad" (Psalm 16:8–9, NIV).

BECAUSE THEY WANT TO ATTRACT FRIENDS

Some people actually believe that if you flash around a bunch of money, you will get a lot of dates or attract a lot of friends. Ah, but what sort of dates? What kind of "friends"?

"Wealth brings many friends, but a poor man's friend deserts him" (Proverbs 19:4, NIV).

I'm so glad Joyce didn't marry me for my money. It's

nice to know that this beautiful woman wasn't attracted to me because of my bank account or stock portfolio. It might have been for my brand-new green VW Bug, but it wasn't for my money.

If she even imagined that I had a stash tucked away somewhere, the first three years of our marriage would have cured her. In our first apartment we slept on the floor on a twin mattress we shoved up against the wall. The bedroom was just big enough to let us walk around that little mattress. To flush the toilet, you had to hit the wall. Don't ask why; that's the way it worked. I still find myself wanting to bang on the bathroom wall now and then, just for old times' sake.

No, there weren't many fattened oxen on the dinner table. But there was love around that little table, and laughter, too. The Lord provided for us in beautiful ways. They were great years, and we wouldn't trade them for a million-dollar lottery ticket.

BECAUSE WE'VE FORGOTTEN ABOUT GOD'S PROMISE OF CARE

Do you know what Joyce and I sensed the Lord telling us in those early years? It's the same thing He tells us today: "I want to provide for you. Work hard, meet your obligations, and do everything you need to do, but please remember that your future rests in My provision for you." Isn't that the message of God's Son? Please read the next paragraphs very carefully.

> "Therefore I say to you, do not worry about your life, what you will eat or what you will drink; nor about your body, what you will put on. Is not life more than food and the body more than clothing? Look at the birds of the air, for they neither sow nor reap nor gather into barns; yet your heavenly Father feeds them. Are you not of more value than they?... For after all these things the Gentiles seek. For your heavenly Father knows that you need all these things. But seek first the kingdom of God and His right-eousness, and all these things shall be added to you." (Matthew 6:25–26, 32–33)

When you know that God is your Provider, it changes everything. Your heart. The way you live. And it certainly changes the way you view your possessions.

TRUST IN GOD AND BE SATISFIED

The only way you can keep this commandment is to make a decision to be satisfied. The book of Hebrews says this very pointedly:

Let your character be free from the love of money, being content with what you have; for He Himself has said, "I will never desert you, nor will I ever forsake you," so that we confidently say, "The LORD is my helper, I will not be afraid. What shall man do to me?" (Hebrews 13:5–6, NASB)

The world will find every way it can to charge you more and give you less. There will be fewer crackers in the box, fewer potato chips in the bag, and less meat in the hamburger.

But the Lord says to us, "Don't you worry about that. And don't steal or spend all of your energy trying to scheme and manipulate things to your own advantage. Because if you obey My Word, I'll provide for your every need all the days of your life."

Chapter 10

WORDS THAT WOUND, WORDS THAT HEAL

*"You shall not bear false witness
against your neighbor."*

Exodus 20:16

A MIDDLE-AGED PASTOR in a small farming community in the Midwest had been falsely accused. A vicious, scandalous story swept through town like a prairie fire.

"Have you heard about the pastor?"

"Can you believe it? He oughta leave town!"

"You'd never think such a thing to look at him, would you?"

"His poor wife."

After a time, however, the rumor was found to be just that. But many people had believed every word and were now reluctant to revise their opinions.

Some time later, the couple who had spread the false tale came under conviction and went to the pastor to apologize. "Of course I will forgive you," he replied gravely. "But could I ask you to do something for me? Something that might seem rather strange at first?"

Could you gather up all the feathers and bring them back?

The couple readily agreed.

"All right," he said, "I would like you to go home and butcher one of your chickens. Pluck all of its feathers and put them in a bag. Could you do that for me?"

They nodded yes; they could certainly do that. But it seemed so strange. Was the man asking for a chicken?

"Next," the pastor went on, "I'd like you to go throughout the town and scatter some of the feathers at each corner. Then take what's left and climb to the top of the water tower and scatter those to the wind. Could you do those things?"

They were mystified, but agreed.

"Fine," the pastor said, "just fine." But as the couple

turned to leave, he called them back.

"Just one more thing. After you've finished scattering all the feathers, I'd like you to go back through town and gather them all up again. Okay? Make sure you pick up every one and put them all back in the bag. Please be careful that none of the feathers are missing, and bring the bag back to me. Could you do that for me?"

The couple just looked at him. "Pastor, that's impossible," the man said. "They'll be all over three counties by then."

The pastor didn't say a word, and slowly the truth began to dawn.

WORDS THAT SHAPE LIVES

We damage, damn, and destroy people when we speak untrue words about them. Jesus Himself felt their unjust sting. The religious leaders of His day looked for false evidence to use against Him. They searched for anything that could undercut His reputation. Why? Because He had the esteem and attention of the public. So they looked to destroy Him any way they could, knowing that words were every bit as destructive as sharp stones.

But I believe that bearing false witness goes well beyond bringing faulty evidence into a judicial setting. Sometimes I want to shout it out loud from a rooftop: Life and death are in the power of the tongue! What you say, what you do not say, and how you say something will either build an individual up, board by board, or tear that person down into a pile of rubble.

Is tearing somebody down with words bearing false witness? It certainly is. When we are not walking in the power of God's Spirit, false, damaging, crippling words will flow right out of our old fleshly nature—words we cannot call back, no matter how we long to. And God takes such matters seriously.

> Therefore each of you must put off falsehood and speak truthfully to his neighbor.... Do not let any unwholesome talk come out of your mouths, but only what is helpful for building others up according to their needs, that it may benefit those who listen. And do not grieve the Holy Spirit of God. (Ephesians 4:25, 29–30, NIV)

A friend of mine found out, after the fact, that he and his family had been living next door to an arsonist for several years. The fellow would deliberately set terrible forest fires, then come home in the evening, wave at his neighbors, thumb through his mail, and walk into the house. The fires were horribly destructive, burning beautiful stands of timber and luxury homes. He was eventually jailed, but the thought of having lived next to such a person gave my friend a funny feeling.

Imagine, living next to an arsonist! Yet the truth is, many of us do live next to arsonists. Or maybe…that's who we are. James writes: "A whole forest can be set ablaze by a tiny spark of fire, and the tongue is a fire, a whole world of evil. It is set within our bodily members but it can poison the whole body, it can set the whole of life ablaze, fed with the fires of hell" (James 3:5–6, Phillips).

There are those who start terrible, raging fires with their words. It may be only a tiny spark here and there—something no bigger than a single match. But what can one match do? It can wipe away the work of generations. It can devastate ten thousand lives.

God intended our words to bring counsel, encouragement, and blessing. Proverbs 16:24 (NIV) says, "Pleasant words are a honeycomb, sweet to the soul and healing to the bones."

A WITNESS TO THE WORLD

God intends for the words of His church to touch the world. And when we speak lovingly and respectfully to one another, we literally identify ourselves as His disciples. God knew that loving words, matched with loving deeds, would be the greatest source of evangelism.

Paul wrote: "Live wisely among those who are not Christians.... Let your conversation be gracious and effective so that you will have the right answer for everyone" (Colossians 4:5–6, NLT).

But what if I am one of those who has dropped matches in the wrong places? What if I have spread poisonous cynicism or toxic criticism? How can I get my tongue back under control?

REALIZE THAT ONLY GOD
CAN CHANGE THE WAY YOU SPEAK

Every now and then you read a horrible story of a child mauled by some wild animal that had supposedly been domesticated. "It was tame!" the keepers protest. "It never hurt anyone else." But somehow, this "tamed" cougar, leopard, or wolf suddenly reverted back to an old instinct—to lash out, to maim, to kill.

Our tongue has that same awful potential. Just when we think we have our mouths under control, something will set us off, and we will maul someone with angry or bitter words.

You'll never be able to train your tongue to bring life instead of death. Only God can turn bitter water sweet. The people of Israel learned that lesson just a short time before they received the Ten Commandments. They came to a place called Marah and found the water there too bitter to drink. And what happened? They became bitter and murmured against Moses. "So he cried out to the LORD, and the LORD showed him a tree; and when he cast it into the waters, the waters were made sweet" (Exodus 15:25).

God is in the business of turning the bitter water sweet in our lives. You and I can add flavoring to try to disguise the bitter taste, but we cannot make it pure and sweet. He can. Because Jesus tasted the bitterness of suffering and death for us, we can experience life as pure and sweet as the water from an artesian spring. God showed Moses a tree in that place of bitterness, and He shows us a tree as well…the cross of Jesus Christ.

RESPOND TO THE HOLY SPIRIT'S PROMPTINGS

Have you ever wanted to tell someone something, yet knew you really shouldn't?

I was speaking to a woman on our staff recently and said, "You know, I probably shouldn't tell you this…" Then she looked at me and said, "Well then, I guess you'd better not."

That set me back on my heels! I smiled, kept my lip buttoned, and walked away. I already respected that lady a great deal, and now I respect her even more. God used her to remind me how I ought to handle privileged information.

We need to make conscious decisions to respond to

those inner whispers of God's Spirit. Whenever the Lord speaks to us, we need to act on His promptings right away. Because if you say what you know you shouldn't say, someone will be hurt or damaged. You'll realize that you have seized control of your own life again—and grieved the Spirit of the Lord.

BE ACCOUNTABLE

Be accountable to the Holy Spirit. When He says "Watch it," then watch it. When He says "Don't," then don't. When He says "Bite your tongue," then put your teeth into it. You'll feel that nudge and you'll think, *I shouldn't be saying this.*

Listen to that voice, even if it makes for an awkward moment or two. Even if you come off looking a little silly or overly sensitive. What is that in comparison to pleasing God?

Life and death are in the power of the tongue.

But be accountable to someone else, too. When you know you've messed up, tell that friend or prayer partner about it. Say, "You know, I told you I wasn't going to do this anymore, but I just opened my mouth, and what came out wasn't sweetness and light. Would you please pray for me? I don't want to be this way anymore." Every time you admit your sin and seek your friend's prayers, you are growing toward Christlikeness.

CRY OUT FOR HELP

Psalm 19:14 says, "Let the words of my mouth and the meditation of my heart be acceptable in Your sight, O LORD, my strength and my redeemer."

This Lord is the same One who swoops down and bears us up on eagles' wings. This is the God who creates a way and provides for every need—even in an empty desert. Why would He not give us the strength and ability we need to walk in His commands and obey His Word?

RECOMMIT YOUR LIFE
TO WORSHIP AND PRAISE

The first thing I do when I get on my knees is remind God that I know who He is. "You're my Father, my refuge, my redeemer. You're the One who lives within me, the author and finisher of my faith. I praise You. I thank You for being so good." And then I get into all the stuff I need and all the things that concern my heart, just as you do. But when I'm just about finished, I always go back to praise.

Praise is the thing I want to have fresh in my memory when I get up and walk away. I want to remember whom I've been conversing with. I've been talking to the One who can do anything, fix anything, change anything. I've given it all to Him, so now I can walk away saying, "God, thank You for letting me be with You. I praise You and bless You."

When your mouth is filled with gratitude and thanks-giving, there simply won't be room for false or cynical words. When your heart is overflowing with praise, you can climb to the top of a water tower, spread your praise to the winds, and never, never find yourself wishing you could call those words back.

Chapter 11

TRUE
CONTENTMENT

"You shall not covet."

EXODUS 20:17

COULD YOU HANDLE A GLIMPSE of Ron Mehl's dark side?

Here's the truth, and it isn't pretty.

I have an unhealthy attraction to briefcases. What can I say? Some people study faces at airport gates. I study briefcases. And when I see something sleek and professional, my mouth starts to water. When I hear those golden snaps popping open, I turn and stare in spite of myself.

Recently, I'd been whining around home before Christmas, trying to convince my family to be sensitive to my needs and buy me a certain briefcase. I was sure that if I just had that briefcase, I would be a contented man at last.

So they bought it for me. The very one I'd longed for. I was elated! But a few days later, I saw one I liked even better. And somehow, that took some of the shine off mine. I felt like a second-class citizen when I walked through the airport.

You see? Once you start coveting, you're never satisfied. Contentment slips out the back door. And contentment, I believe, is the bottom line of this final commandment.

God knows very well what happens to people when they are caught up in envy. What God really intends for us is that we would be content with who we are and what we have. Content with Him.

A covetous individual tends to see the world in terms of how it benefits him. Short-term satisfaction elbows out long-term goals and deeply held values. But God sees the big picture while we see only a tiny slice, often colored with "me."

I remember a time when I was leaving a conference

for home. On that morning I prayed, *Lord, You know how much I want to get home. As a personal favor, please don't let there be any delays at the airport.*

But when I arrived at the gate, guess what? My flight had been delayed for more than an hour. I was so disappointed. Hadn't the Lord heard me that morning? Was I tuned in on the wrong wavelength? I remember thinking, *Why does this always happen to me? I miss my family so much. I'll bet nobody in this airport loves their family like I do.*

But what happened next jarred me.

I saw a young man run down the concourse, struggling with his bags. He ran right up to where I was waiting, looked at the new departure time, and said, "Oh, thank God!" And then he told the agent, "My little boy was struck by a car. He's in serious condition. My wife's alone with him at the hospital."

Once you start coveting, your're never satisfied.

I sat there and thought, *Lord, I'm so glad You didn't answer my selfish prayer.* God used that little incident to help me see how often I'm driven by a desire to meet my needs, rather than looking around and considering that other people have needs, too.

The fact is, God knows exactly what you and I need. He knows when and how much. And He has a way of seeing that we receive what we need at just the right time…not our time, perhaps, but the right time.

WHAT WE COVET WILL NOT LAST

The very things people long to hold in their hands will slip between their fingers. Second Corinthians 4:18 (NIV) says:

> So we fix our eyes not on what is seen, but on what is unseen. For what is seen is temporary, but what is unseen is eternal.

The Lord is saying, "Life on earth is uncertain and fragile enough as it is; I want you to concentrate on what will last."

I've told you about the bedroom in our first apartment. We had only one twin-size mattress. Joyce was so tiny that I would push it against the wall so I wouldn't kick her out of bed by accident. Would I have been happier in a palatial master bedroom in a giant bed with silk sheets? Not a chance! I wouldn't trade those memories for anything.

WHAT WE COVET WILL BE A BURDEN

If you don't believe that, read Psalm 51. David coveted his neighbor's wife. And so he took her. David wrote

Psalm 51 in the aftermath, and they are the words of a broken man who longed with all his heart to turn back the clock. But he could not. David watched his family sink into heartbreak and ruin. Rape, murder, incest, rebellion…it never stopped.

David had thought, *There's an empty place inside me; if I could just possess Uriah's wife, I would be satisfied and fulfilled.* Instead, David had his heart shattered into ten thousand pieces.

God knows how burdensome the things we covet can become. Their weight can distract us and squeeze all the joy out of life.

COVETOUSNESS IS DESTRUCTIVE

No one said it more clearly than Paul to his young friend Timothy:

> People who want to get rich fall into temptation and a trap and into many foolish and harmful desires that plunge men into ruin and destruction. For the love of money is a root of all kinds of evil. (1 Timothy 6:9–10, NIV)

Paul says that people who long to be rich soon do all kinds of wrong things to get more money. Some counselors say the number one cause of divorce today is finances. Unwise spending becomes a breeding ground for arguments and fights. Covetousness brings destruction, divorce, and death.

COVETOUSNESS IS DECEPTIVE

In Luke 12:15 (NIV), Jesus says: "Watch out! Be on your guard against all kinds of greed; a man's life does not consist in the abundance of his possessions."

Do we truly believe that? Today's sophisticated marketers spend billions of dollars and work around the clock for one purpose: to make you dissatisfied with what you have. With all their skill, talent, and training, they seek to convince you and I that if we would just buy this or possess that, we'd find more happiness and security.

Is "new" really better? I think my favorite car of all during my growing-up years was our family's old Chevy station wagon. The Brown Beauty. I can still remember all nine of us dashing madly to the car to claim the front seat. Failing that, we'd grab the door handle and holler, "Window! Window! I get the window!" We'd joke and laugh and fight in the backseats. And Mom would draw lines so we wouldn't invade one another's territories.

Our value does not spring from what we wear, what we drive, or where we live.

We even ate our lunches in that car. My friends

would always brag about their families' big expensive cars. But their cars weren't as much fun because before you got in, you had to clean off your shoes. And you couldn't eat candy or ice cream.

Our value does not lie in what we possess. It doesn't spring from what we wear, what we drive, or where we live. Our value is wrapped up in the amazing fact that Jesus Christ, the mighty Son of God and Creator of the world, loved us enough to pay the price for our salvation.

Can a husband and wife who delight in one another enjoy a dinner of hot dogs and beans by candlelight as much as stuffed pheasant with plum sauce in some five-star restaurant? Can you tell time with a ten-dollar Timex as well as a thousand-dollar Rolex?

Oh, how disappointed and dissatisfied we can become when we realize that the things we finally possess after long waiting are not the things that bring satisfaction or lasting contentment.

CONTENTMENT IS A PROCESS

In Philippians 4:11 (NIV), Paul writes: "I have learned to be content whatever the circumstances." Please note that. Paul learned contentment from the Lord. It didn't happen overnight.

Attitude is everything; if we don't learn to be content, we'll face the same circumstances again and again.

That's why the children of Israel wandered for forty years in the Sinai wilderness. Around and around, year after year, seeing the same scrawny trees, the same boring rocks, the same shriveled-up bushes. That's why you hear yourself say, "Well, here we go again. We've gone through this a million times."

The apostle wrote: "I once thought all these things were so very important, but now I consider them worthless because of what Christ has done. Yes, everything else is worthless when compared with…knowing Christ Jesus my Lord. I have discarded everything else, counting it all as garbage" (Philippians 3:7–8, NLT).

Once Paul found the true artesian spring of contentment, everything else tasted like flat Coke.

TRUE CONTENTMENT BRINGS PEACE

People lust after success and possessions yet pay a tremendous price in their family and their home. They want more and more but are never satisfied.

Is it wrong to want success in your life? "Is that a problem," you ask? No, I hope you are as successful as you can be. But if that's the goal of your life, I will tell you that when you get there (wherever "there" may be), it won't be enough.

I have a friend, Ron Rearick, who, before he became a Christian, extorted a million dollars from United

Airlines. He picked up the money at the drop site and sat in his car, counting the bundles. One million dollars. But the only thought that kept going through his mind that day was, *This isn't enough. I should have asked for more.*

When I say that contentment brings peace, I mean that in those personal times with God—even in the midst of difficult, heartbreaking circumstances—you and I learn true contentment. Because we know God is going to take care of everything. He's going to work everything out. We know that.

Whatever your circumstance today—this very moment—He can make your cup overflow. Even if you drive an old brown station wagon.

Even if you carry last year's briefcase.

Chapter 12

WHOEVER TAKES THE SON

*"He who believes in the Son has everlasting life;
and he who does not believe the Son
shall not see life."*

JOHN 3:36

EARLIER WE SAID THAT GOD'S WORD is like a fence
that separates us from danger. Maybe so, but in our quiet
moments do we sit back and meditate on white pickets
and barbed wire? Probably not. But we would meditate
on a love letter from the dearest person in our lives,
wouldn't we?

That's what I've been trying to demonstrate. More than anything else, the Ten Commandments are a full-hearted love letter from God. A fence? Yes, that too. But listen for a moment to the excitement—the passion—in the psalmist's heart as he describes his experience with the commands of God's Word:

> I meditate on your precepts and consider your
> ways.
> I delight in your decrees; I will not neglect your
> word....
> My soul is consumed with longing for your laws
> at all times....
> Your statutes are my delight; they are my coun-
> selors.
> (Psalm 119:15–16, 20, 24, NIV)

Why should I love His commands? Why should I love those things with all of my heart?

BECAUSE HIS WORD WILL KEEP ME FROM DISASTER

My friend Larry told me about one of the first bike rides he attempted with his young son, Matthew. Going down a hill near their home, little Matt lost control. When he crashed, Matt went over the handlebars, landed on his head, and scooted along the asphalt for several feet…on the top of his helmet.

When Matt got up, Larry looked at the helmet and saw that its top—and not the top of his son's head!—had been badly scraped and scored by the rough asphalt. How do you think Larry felt about that helmet? He loved that helmet. He kissed it. He valued and honored that helmet, and used it as an object lesson for his boy.

A person who resists, scorns, and rejects God's Word will meet with destruction. I wish I could say it in a nicer way, but as a pastor, I see it all the time. People say, "I don't need God, and I don't need His Word. I don't care about His requirements. I don't care to hear His warnings. I'll do what I want." That person's life will come to disaster in one way or another, and God's Word is not shy about saying so.

BECAUSE HIS WORD BRINGS DEEP SATISFACTION

When you're hiking in the wilderness, you're foolish if you don't bring along a map and a compass. Those items are as basic as a canteen and waterproof matches. In the same way, without the direction and counsel of God's Word, you will end up wandering around in circles. You will waste your life.

There are people who say, "Well, I don't respond to

God's love and His commands, and look how well-off I am. Look at how much I've achieved." I'm not suggesting that these people couldn't have achieved financial success apart from the Word, but they will never be satisfied. In the end they will say, "I've accumulated all this, but I've never really found a purpose for living. I've never found out why I'm here or what God wanted me to do with my life." That's a pretty desolate thing to realize as you approach the end of your days.

BECAUSE HIS WORD PROVIDES A FOUNDATION FOR YOUR LIFE

In a small Kansas town a number of years ago, many were gathered in the high school gymnasium for a basketball game. Things were going well for the home team, but what happened at halftime changed that little town forever.

A person who resists and rejects God's Word will meet with destruction.

The town was suddenly rocked by a powerful explosion, the kind you feel deep in your chest. Everyone ran outside. The town's massive grain elevator had fallen across a small nursery school. Five little children died.

What could have caused such a shocking event? After a close inspection, investigators discovered that termites had eaten out the heart of the structure, leaving only an empty shell. Subtle devastation, completely hidden from the eye.

I often wonder if that isn't what happens to the lives of those who disregard God's loving instructions to them. God's intended that His Word would be the foundation of our lives. Psalm 19:7 reaffirms this over and over: "The testimony of the LORD is sure, making wise the simple."

The word *simple* means inability to distinguish between good and bad, right and wrong. How appropriate for today, when so many lines are deliberately blurred. The Lord says, "If you will walk in obedience to My commands, you will become an extremely wise person, although you once were naive or undiscerning."

EAGLES' WINGS

"I bore them on eagles' wings," the Lord reminded Moses.

He still does. He's still swooping down and plucking us out of free fall, soaring into the heavens while we hang on for the ride. Do you know why? Because we can't live by these commands in our own strength. We can't do it. As many have correctly said, the Christian life isn't difficult; it's impossible. Only by His grace and His aid can we succeed.

Consider the widowed, wealthy man who shared with his son a passion for collecting art. Together they traveled the world, adding only the finest treasures to their collection. Priceless works by Picasso, van Gogh, Monet, and many others adorned the walls of the family estate.

As winter approached one year, war engulfed the nation and the young man left to serve his country. After a few weeks, his father received a telegram. The young man had died while attempting to evacuate a wounded fellow soldier.

Distraught and lonely, the old man faced the upcoming Christmas holidays with dread. What was left to celebrate? His joy was gone.

Early on Christmas morning, a knock on the door awakened the grieving man. As he walked to the door, the masterpieces of art on the walls seemed to mock him. Of what value were they without his son to share their beauty?

He's still swooping down and plucking us out of free fall, soaring into the heavens while we hang on for the ride.

Opening the door, he saw a young man in uniform with a large package in his hands. "I was a friend to your son," he said. "As a matter of fact, I was the one he was rescuing when he died. May I come in? I have something to show you."

The soldier told of how the man's son had talked so

much about art and the joy of collecting masterpieces alongside his father. "I'm something of an artist myself," the soldier said shyly. "And, well, I wanted you to have this."

As the old man unwrapped the package, he revealed a portrait of his son. Though the world would never consider it a work of genius, the painting somehow captured the young man's likeness. Overcome with emotion, the man thanked the soldier, promising to hang the picture above his fireplace.

A few hours later the old man set about his task. True to his word, he put the painting above the fireplace, pushing aside a fortune in classic artworks. The old man sat in his chair and spent Christmas day gazing at the gift.

During the days and weeks that followed, the man gradually realized that even though his son was no longer with him, the boy would live on because of those he had touched. His son had rescued dozens of wounded soldiers before a bullet had cut him down.

Fatherly pride and satisfaction began to ease the old man's grief. The painting of his son soon became his most prized possession. He told his neighbors it was the greatest gift he had ever received.

The following spring, the old man passed away. With the famous collector's passing, the art world eagerly anticipated a great auction. According to the collector's will, all of the works would be auctioned on Christmas Day, the day he had received the greatest gift.

The day soon arrived, and art dealers from around the world gathered. Dreams would be fulfilled this day; many would soon claim, "I have the greatest collection." The auction began, however, with a painting that was not on any museum's list.

It was the simple portrait of a young soldier…the collector's son.

The auctioneer asked for an opening bid, but the room was silent. "Who will open with a bid of one hundred dollars?" he asked. Minutes passed and no one spoke. From the back of the room came a gruff voice, "Who cares about that? It's just a picture of his son." More voices echoed in agreement. "Let's forget about it and move on to the good stuff."

"No," the auctioneer replied. "We have to sell this one first."

Finally, a neighbor of the old man spoke. "Will you take ten dollars for the painting? That's all I can spare. I knew the boy, so I'd like to have it."

"I have ten dollars," called the auctioneer. "Will anyone go higher?" After more silence, the auctioneer said, "Going once; going twice; sold!" The gavel fell. Cheers filled the room and someone exclaimed, "Now we can get on with it."

But at that moment, the auctioneer looked up at the audience and quietly announced that the auction was over. Stunned disbelief blanketed the room. Finally someone spoke up. "What do you mean, it's over? We didn't come here for a picture of some old guy's son! What about all of these paintings? There are millions of dollars' worth of art here! What's going on?"

The auctioneer replied, "It's very simple. According to the will of the father, whoever takes the son...gets it all."

And so it is.

The publisher and author would love to hear your comments about this book. *Please contact us at:* www.lifechangebooks.com

Notes

1. C. S. Lewis, *The Magician's Nephew* (New York, N.Y.: Harper Collins Publishers, Inc., 1955), 44.